VAUX
LE
VICOMTE

"*This* was the estate I regarded as my principal seat, and where I intended to leave some traces of the status I had enjoyed."
These lines were written from the prison he was never to leave alive, by Nicolas Fouquet, the former Lord High Treasurer of France.

The architectural masterpiece of Vaux-le-Vicomte, the unfailing friendship of the poet La Fontaine and a famous political trial have kept alive the memory of this outstanding man.

In spite of wars and revolutions, and despite the changes of fashion of the intervening three hundred years of European history, the estate of Vaux has been preserved intact to the present day.

This most unusual survival is due to the determination of men from all walks of life, who, in each succeeding generation, have been inspired and united by a common passion for Vaux-le-Vicomte : its owners, architects, masons, gardeners, sculptors, painters, carpenters, not to mention La Fontaine, Voltaire, Anatole France, and Pierre de Nolhac, all of whom have borne witness to the magical attraction of this place.

I sincerely hope that this estate, preserved complete in its original beauty, will afford you the same delight that it has given all those who have spent here only a few hours, or have lived here for years : the pleasure to be found in a perfect work of human endeavour.

COUNT PATRICE DE VOGÜÉ

Robert Nanteuil,
Portrait of Nicolas Fouquet,
vicomte de Vaux, 1661
Nicolas Fouquet, born in 1615 to
a family originating from Anjou,
was the son of a maître des
requêtes (State Counsel),
François Fouquet, and Marie
de Maupeou, who also came
from a family associated with
the Parlement (French courts
of justice). After studying
at the Jesuit college in Clermont,
Nicolas in turn bought an office
as maître des requêtes, and in
1640 he married Louise Fourché.
Fouquet became Public
Prosecutor to the Parlement in
1650; during the Fronde period
(1648-1652) he remained loyal
both to the king and to Mazarin
who was looking after
government affairs during
the king's minority. In 1651 he
remarried, to Marie-Madeleine
de Castille, and two years later
he was appointed
Superintendent of Finances,
which meant he was Chancelor
of the Exchequer as well as Lord
High-treasurer to the kingdom.
On Mazarin's death in 1661,
it was his ambition to become
First Minister. He was reckoning
without Colbert, who convinced
the king that Fouquet was
misappropriating public funds,
and even plotting against him.
Colbert achieved his objective as
the Superintendent was arrested
the very same year.

The Fouquet coat of arms
The emblem of the Fouquet
family was derived from the
word "fouquet" which is the
word for squirrel in Anjou,
the region the family came
from. The small climbing
animal likewise justified the
motto chosen by Nicolas's
father, François Fouquet,
Quo non ascendet?
This emblem can be found
on many of surfaces at the
château, on the façades or
in the inside rooms,
accompanied by lions which
are featured on the family
coat-of-arms.

The monogram
of the Fouquets
Carved on the garden façade
of the château, these two
intertwined Fs represent
the monogram of Fouquet,
which is sometimes traversed
by an arrow, the symbol
of married love.
The couple had four children,
the eldest of whom
recovered his title and land
only twelve years after
his father's arrest.

When the last lights of the sumptuous festivity held on 17 August 1661 were extinguished in the gardens of Vaux, when the sound of the guests' horses had faded behind the nearby woods, Nicolas Fouquet had every reason to think that he was favoured by the gods: the king himself, Louis XIV, had just trodden on the marble floors and parterres of his brand new château, complimenting his Superintendent of Finances on it. Yet again fortune had favoured the bold: Fouquet was at the apex of power, the finest intellects and greatest talents in the kingdom had been assembled beneath his gilded ceilings. *Quo non ascendet?* as his family motto said,

Bust of Louis XIV
This bust executed in 1665 in a style close to that of Bernini shows the king at the age of twenty-seven, dominating and jealous of his power. Four years previously he had been present at Vaux as the wealth of his Superintendent was first conspicuously displayed. If the elimination of Fouquet was not dictated by envy, it certainly corresponds to the king's desire

"What heights might he not reach?" The answer came like a thunderbolt less than a month later; on 5 September Fouquet was arrested and cast into prison where he would remain until his death in 1680. Never again would he see the magnificent château to which he had devoted all his taste and intelligence, and which remains one of the supreme feats of seventeenth-century French architecture.

For the château of Vaux really is the achievement of one man: the place, the architect, the painters, the "gardeners", Nicolas Fouquet had chosen them all.

It had taken five years to build the château on a small manorial estate purchased in 1641 where two small valleys converged, with money he had inherited from his father and his first wife, Louise Fourché, who had died one year after their marriage. To provide full scope for the scheme, 500 hectares had been cleared, razing the old château as

well as the village of Vaux and two nearby hamlets. The buildings, gardens and waterfalls were laid out along an axis measuring almost two miles from north to south. Nothing was too grand, nothing too fine for the Superintendent, who swallowed up large sums on his project, so attracting the thunderbolts of the king's jealousy. Later on the judges would have a fine time at his trial accusing him of having misappropriated money belonging to the state for his own profit, and enriching himself unduly. Everything seemed to condemn him. But first and foremost he upset the scheme of things. For over and above his wealth and his appetite for power, Fouquet was a master of the art of living: Vaux was the brilliant but fatal demonstration of that mastery.

to take over the running of the kingdom himself : 1661 was the year when Mazarin died, when Louis XIV decided to rule personally, and he regarded Nicolas Fouquet's power as excessive. But no doubt it was his own desire for unparalleled fame that led him to turn Versailles into such a splendid palace, calling on the three brilliant builders employed at Vaux-le-Vicomte: Le Vau, Le Brun and Le Nôtre.

*Portrait of Charles Le Brun
(1619-1690) after Nicolas
de Largillière*
*When Nicolas Fouquet engaged
him to decorate his château,
Le Brun was first and foremost
a painter, and had not revealed
the full measure of his talent.
Here at Vaux he became a true
chief designer, providing
drawings not only for
the paintings but also for
the decorative sculptures
in most of the rooms, inspired
by the Italianate style he had
absorbed in Rome. He was
assisted by talented sculptors
such as Michel Anguier,
François Girardon and Mathieu
Lespagnandel. Unfortunately Le
Brun was not able to complete
his major undertaking at Vaux:
the decorative programme
of the Salon, which has come
down to us only in the form
of drawings of the scheme.*

To implement his huge scheme for a château successfully, Nicolas Fouquet called on three men of his own generation : the architect Louis Le Vau, the painter Charles Le Brun, and the gardener André Le Nôtre. While the talent of the first two was recognized, none of the three had yet achieved the celebrity which the construction, decoration and gardens of Versailles would later bring.

Work on the site started in 1656. It took a year to complete the masonry and joinery work, and the roof went on in 1657; the floors and wainscoting were installed a few months later, and in September 1658 Charles Le Brun arrived at Vaux to work on the interior decoration. In spite of the fast pace of the work, not everything was finished three years later when Fouquet was arrested, but the grandiose ambition of the builders of Vaux-le-Vicomte had been achieved in full.

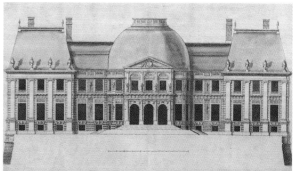

Section through the
vestibule and the Salon,
measured drawing by
Rodolphe Pfnor, 1888
Louis Le Vau can be considered
to have introduced architectural
ideas borrowed from Italy
to France, although he never
went there: the Salon covered
with a rotunda is a stroke of
genius which was to have many
imitators. Above the dome
there is a lantern from which
a thousand rockets were fired
on 17 August 1661; as they fell
back to earth they formed
a virtual vault of fire.

In keeping with a tradition that was soon to disappear, the château was built on a platform of earth surrounded by water-filled moats. A wide courtyard with two terraces on either side stands in front of the château entrance, which is approached by a huge flight of steps. On the garden side we again find these successive terraces leading in a downward sweep towards the parterres, so emphasizing the elevated position of the building.

It is believed to be Le Nôtre who conceived the axial composition of the château and the gardens, so creating an exceptional perspective. But Le Vau must be given credit for the design of the house with its massed plan, for the double-depth building, and first and foremost – an example that would be widely imitated – for inventing the rotunda, several storeys high, containing an Italian-style Salon in place of the traditional gallery found in earlier French châteaux.

The *piano nobile* henceforth became the ground floor. The reception rooms were organized around the *sallon* (from the Italian *sallone*), no longer around a monumental stairway; at Vaux that was replaced by two modest staircases consigned to either side of the vestibule. The three openings of this central room were originally enclosed only by railings, opening on to the garden. The king's suite of rooms, always provided in a grand house, and Fouquet's were symmetrical, each consisting of an antechamber, a main room and a study; they were intended for public receptions.

The private suites of rooms and the chapel were on the first floor, while the basement contained the kitchen, pantry, bedrooms and cellar.

Scheme by Louis Le Vau,
courtyard elevation and
garden elevation
These schemes drawn by
Le Vau in 1656 do not
completely correspond to
the château as it was finally
built, since the brick and stone
course work planned was
replaced by just stone,
regarded as grander.
Fontainebleau sandstone was
chosen for the wall bases,
and stone from Creil for
the façades. On the other
hand, the general approach
to the building established
by Le Vau remained the same:
a central block with three
projecting parts on the
courtyard side and a rotunda
on the garden side, as well
as the four pavilions.

Concave expanse of wall on the courtyard façade
These curved expanses of wall were intended to soften the reflex angles; they include windows and are enlivened by marble busts on brackets, with the panels above the windows carved in bas-relief to depict the trophies of the arts and sciences. The window lights were originally held by lead cames, not wooden bars which were introduced at a later date.

Moat, and garden façade
The water-filled moat was preserved from the earlier château; it is still crossed today by means of a drawbridge which is in working order, and there are still carp swimming peacefully in the moat. The austere sandstone used for the lower parts of the château is in contrast to the golden hue of the garden façade, constructed of limestone. Above the windows are the monogram of the Fouquets with its two intertwined Fs against a background of olive branches – a symbol of the peace which the Superintendent's benevolent works helped to promote – and the squirrel framed by two lions, the heraldic emblems of the family. The sculpture by Michel Anguier in the foreground has been identified as Justice, but it is not completely certain that it should be so interpreted.

Central projection on the courtyard façade
The entrance to the château from the courtyard, leading into the vestibule, is formed by four rusticated columns with marble medallions between them featuring Roman emperors. In the pediment, putti playing with lions surround a shield on which the coat of arms of the Fouquets with their emblem the squirrel was carved; it was chipped off after the Superintendent's fall from favour, then replaced by the arms of the Choiseul-Praslin family, who became owners of the château in 1764. Above, Apollo and Rhea, two figures sculpted by Michel Anguier after a drawing by Charles Le Brun, symbolise Heaven and Earth; the recumbent figures are on the same level as the chapel, located above the vestibule.

*Portrait of André
Le Nôtre (1613-1700)
by Carlo Maratta*
Le Nôtre worked at Vaux for
nearly ten years, arriving in 1653.
He was then forty years old.
While the plan of the garden had
been started well before his
arrival, he made his mark on it,
inventing the famous jardin à la
française on the immense area
entrusted to him by Fouquet,
a style of garden which has been
popular ever since.

*The garden viewed from
the château, drawing
by Israël Silvestre*
Israël Silvestre's drawings
are the primary source of
information about the gardens
at Vaux, and are believed to
predate 1660. This particular
one lets us see that the ground
had only recently been
landscaped from amidst the
surrounding plains of the Brie
region, as can be seen by the
modest stature of the trees. In
the centre we see the parterres
de broderie, on the left the
parterre de la Couronne, and
on the right the parterre de
fleurs, which has not yet
been reinstated.

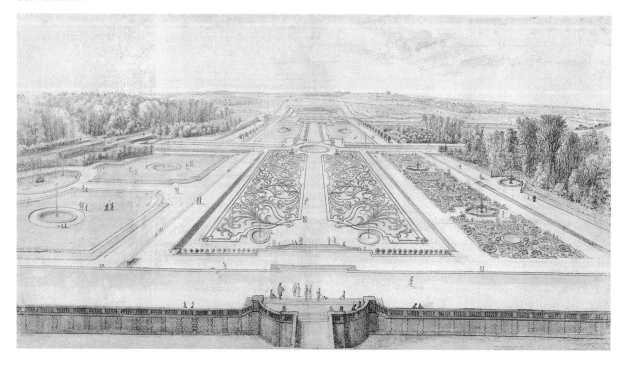

From the terrace of the château on the garden side there is a superb perspective which Madame de Scudéry described enthusiastically in *Clélie*: "From this place you can see such a great and vast expanse of different beds, so many large and beautiful paths, so many gushing fountains, and so many beautiful objects that merge through their distance that you hardly know what you are seeing." This novel in which Vaux is featured under the name of Valterre gives some measure of the sophistication of this garden in the seventeenth century, and of the novelty it undoubtedly represented for contemporaries.

Fouquet gave Le Nôtre, not yet known as a gardener, complete freedom of expression, so enabling him for the first time to reveal the full extent of his inventive genius. On this large site the first *jardin à la française* would be born. While we do not know for certain what landscaping had already been carried out on the plot, it is probable that planting had started before Le Nôtre came, but he was responsible for the parterres with their graceful arabesques, and the subtle succession of sheets of water and waterfalls.

Of course the garden we see today is not three centuries old: it is the product of a determined project to restore it, embarked upon in 1875 by Alfred Sommier, who bought the château surrounded by derelict land. It took fifty years to reinstate it as it had been; fortunately the outlines had been preserved in Israël Sylvestre's drawings and engravings, made when the garden was at its most splendid.

The garden viewed from the terrace
Beyond the drawbridge there is a perspective extending 1500 metres which seems to dissolve into the distant tree-tops. At the foot of the steps, the first garden has parterres de broderie (a type of knot garden), which used sometimes to be called "tapis de turquerie" (Turkish carpet) because of the oriental inspiration of the motifs; they are created from pruned box, sand, charcoal and crushed brick, the latter ingredient explaining the red colour. On the same axis as these first beds, we can see the Rond d'eau, a circular pond encircled by statues.

Nicolas Fouquet certainly did not lack intelligence, daring or skill: his brilliant career and rapid advancement were proof of this. But in his case they were combined with an exceptional aesthetic sense, a liking for Latin poetry and ingenious mottoes, a love of beauty and courtly pursuits. "Everyone knows that this great minister is no less the superintendent of literature than of finances; that his house is as open to people of intellect as to businessmen," Pierre Corneille wrote in 1659.

For Fouquet Vaux was to be the privileged resort of a peace dedicated to literature and the arts, the meeting-place for all the talents and fine intellects France could muster. As a patron he granted pensions to writers and scholars. And while he showered artists with gifts and commissions, he also won their friendship. They would all remember this. When the wheel of fortune had turned at the time of his trial, he found sure allies in those artists.

In the forefront of those who enjoyed his protection were La Fontaine, Molière, Corneille and Charles Perrault. La Fontaine wrote *Le Songe de Vaux*, a poem exalting Vaux and its master, while Molière performed *L'École des maris* at the château and was commissioned to write *Les Fâcheux* for the final festivity in August 1661. As well as writers, there were painters such as Poussin – Fouquet bought *La Manne* by Poussin – or Le Brun, and sculptors such as Pierre Puget.

Fouquet also had other close friends around him whose names have now been forgotten, as well as some famous friends: Mme de Scudéry, Scarron, or the marquise de Sévigné; the Superintendent sought her favours – unsuccessfully, so it seems – but her loyalty in his time of trial was unwavering.

Another indication of the Superintendent's love of the arts is his correspondence with his brother Louis, a priest living in Italy, with regard to acquiring pictures and sculptures. Through Louis he purchased three works by Veronese, and some of the marble busts that are now displayed in the Salon.

Finally we are indebted to Fouquet for creating the tapestry workshop at Maincy near the château of Vaux where nearly 300 employees, including nineteen Flemish tapestry makers, worked under Le Brun's supervision. After the Superintendent's downfall, this and other tapestry workshops were transferred to the Gobelins where the tapestries begun at Maincy were completed.

Illumination of the château and gardens
Every Saturday evening in the summer, two thousand candles are lit to recreate the atmosphere of the splendid festivity held on 17 August 1661.

La Fontaine (1621-1695)
After Fouquet had been imprisoned, his protégé La Fontaine dedicated an elegy to him beseeching Louis XIV's clemency: "Come, O Nymphs of Vaux, increase the waves..."

Molière (1622-1673)
The second play by Molière to be performed at Vaux was Les Fâcheux, *written and produced in a fortnight; it gave rise to the comédie-ballet genre as the interludes were used to perform dances.*

Madame de Sévigné (1626-1696)
The famous writer was nine years younger than Fouquet and may have met him because of their families' shared Breton origin. She remained loyal to the Superintendent.

*A*fter his arrest in Nantes on 5 September 1661, Nicolas Fouquet was brought before the Chamber of Justice, and at the end of three years imprisonment in the Bastille he was sentenced to exile. Regarding that sentence as inadequate, Louis XIV changed it to life imprisonment. A rumour identified Fouquet as the mysterious Man in the Iron Mask; it is today regarded as groundless but it was picked up and brilliantly developed by Alexandre Dumas.

Portrait of Field Marshal de Villars, after Hyacinthe Rigaud
The military imprint given by the new owner was evident in the commission to Jean-Baptiste Martin for a series of ten pictures celebrating the general's victories and the installation of canons on the terraces of the outbuildings.

Portrait of César Gabriel de Choiseul, duc de Praslin
The changes introduced by the duc de Praslin, who bought the château in 1764, were basically confined to installing the library and making alterations that increased the convenience of the private rooms.

The Superintendent survived his downfall, cut off from all contact, for over fifteen years in the fortress of Pignerol in the Savoyard Alps, until his death in 1680.

Immediately after Fouquet's arrest, the king had the château of Vaux emptied of its most splendid items: the furniture, tapestries, statues and paintings were transferred to the Louvre and Versailles. Placed under sequestration, the château was not returned to Madame Fouquet until twelve years later. But in 1705, her eldest son having died without an heir, she sold the château to Field Marshal de Villars. His brilliant feats on the battlefields had led to him being made a duke and a peer of the realm by Louis XIV. On becoming a *duché-pairie* (duchy) in 1709 the Vaux estate took the name of Vaux-Villars.

In the reign of Louis XV the château again experienced moments of glory, and Voltaire was one of its guests. The interior refurbishing of some rooms and purchases of furniture date from that period. But his heir was unable to keep up

the estate, and facing financial ruin, he was forced to sell it in 1764 to the duc de Choiseul-Praslin, a diplomat and Minister for the Navy.

Six generations then succeeded one another at the château. Thanks to a ruse by the second duchesse de Praslin who thought up the idea of bequeathing it to the nation, it escaped destruction during the French Revolution. Sporadic restoration work by a few Praslin descendants in the nineteenth century – the roof lantern, the bathroom by Visconti - could not prevent the slow shipwreck of the château, while Le Nôtre's magnificent *jardin à la française* ceased to be maintained, and was replaced by lawns, then left untended when it did not revert to agricultural use. In the mid-nineteenth century a family tragedy led the heirs gradually to abandon the estate, then put it up for auction.

Alfred Sommier
This astute industrialist, the grandson of a baker from the Yonne, made his fortune in sugar refining; he was also an art enthusiast. Struck by the beauty of Vaux and in particular by the work of Le Brun, he bought the château in 1875 to make it his family home, spending huge sums on restoring it. Given the scale of the task his work was not completed in his life time and it has been continued by his descendants, in particular by his great-grandson, the present owner Patrice de Vogüé.

When Alfred Sommier became the owner in July 1875, major work was needed. The architect Destailleurs took on responsibility for restoring the roofs, rebuilding some collapsing internal walls and part of the outbuildings. The château was almost empty, and Alfred Sommier decided to assemble seventeenth-century furniture for it. But the largest and longest task was the reinstatement of the gardens: given the size of the project, his work was not completed, and was continued by his son and daughter-in-law. Today, his great-grandson, Patrice de Vogüé, the present owner of the château, carves on the conservation of this national inheritance.

View of the gardens c. 1875 (on the left) and today
The architect Gabriel-Hippolyte Destailleurs and the landscape gardener Elie Lainé rescued this land from its derelict state, redesigning the beds on the basis of seventeenth-century documents, restoring the fountains, and refilling the pathways with statues.

Engraved version of Charles Le Brun's scheme for the cupola of the Grand Salon
The present decoration of the cupola, the work of Charles Séchan, was painted c. 1840. A very modest sky compared with Le Brun's scheme – engraved by Audran in 1681 –, a splendid profusion of allegorical figures, Apollo, Bacchus, Venus and Mercury, associated with the symbols of the four seasons. In the centre, Mars, Jupiter and Saturn originally surrounded the squirrel of Fouquet, a culminating star replaced here by the royal coat of arms.

PLAN OF THE CHÂTEAU AND GRAND SALON

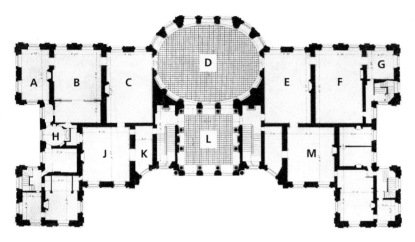

Upper part of the Grand Salon on the vestibule side
The decorative programme of the Grand Salon – incomplete on the evening of the 17 August festivity, and still incomplete – was entirely designed by Le Brun on the theme of a "palace of the Sun" with Apollo/Fouquet as its centre. Below the cornice, the sixteen terms – possibly the work of Girardon – present medallions symbolising the four seasons and the twelve signs of the Zodiac. The significance of the trophies forming the over-window decorations has not been fully explained. The polished stone floor echoes the scheme of the cosmos and the points of reference of a sundial can be seen on it.

Plan of the ground floor
Louis Le Vau's originality in designing this château lay in creating a double-depth building, and above all organizing the layout round the vestibule and the Grand Salon, an oval room 18 m long and 18 m high, with sixteen arches and sixteen Ionic pilasters round the sides.
The ground floor was reserved for the state rooms, all with coved ceilings rather than the "French-style" flat ceiling. Raised in relation to the level of the ground, it provides a wide view across the gardens.
A-B-C. The king's apartments;
D. Grand Salon ;
E-F-G. Fouquet's apartments;
H. Bathroom; J. Dining-room;
K. Serving area; L. Vestibule ;
M. Large square room.

LARGE SQUARE ROOM

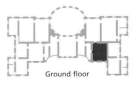

Large square room

While we do not know what its original purpose was, in the time of Field Marshal de Villars, this large room was used for billiards, which justifies the presence there today of the exceptionally large billiard table which occupies its centre, made by Dasson in 1877 in the style of Boulle. In contrast to the other state rooms, the beams and joists are visible here, and have been decorated in the seventeenth-century style. Rather than the wainscoting which dates from the early twentieth century, a set of tapestries telling the Story of Iphigenia covered the walls, a set of six hangings after cartoons by Charles Le Brun which were made at Maincy, near Vaux, a haute lisse tapestry workshop founded by Fouquet. The huge pictures by an anonymous painter depict de Villars's victories which earned him the title of duke and peer of the realm.

As it was unfinished at the time of the 1661 festivities, this room was decorated in a hurry, so it seems, and in the lower part there are still vestiges of paint with the Fouquet monogram. The frieze placed below the ceiling displays a procession of gold-coloured Roman soldiers against a blue background: it is the work of Charles Le Brun, and has been likened to projects he had for a huge Triumph of Constantine: it was never made, but the engravings have been preserved.

THE CHAMBRE DES MUSES

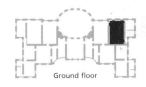

Chambre des Muses, or Fouquet's bedchamber
The state apartment intended for Fouquet, this room owes its name to the nine Muses adorning the coving and ceiling: it is regarded as one of Charles Le Brun's masterpieces. It was in the alcove, slightly raised in relation to the rest of the room, that L'École des maris was performed on 12 July 1660, enacted by Molière himself in the presence of the Superintendent, and with Queen Henrietta Maria of England, Louis XIII's sister, accompanied by her daughter Henrietta, the wife of Monsieur, Louis XIV's brother, among the audience. This alcove, with its ceiling representing Night, was never completed: it was to have been framed by two caryatids and two columns.

Chambre des Muses
The central motif of the ceiling of the room – reversed by the mirror – depicts The Triumph of Fidelity. It features Clio, the muse of History, led by Prudence and followed by Fidelity: a clear reference to Fouquet's stance during the Fronde. In the corner are Thalia, the Muse of comedy, and Melpomene, the Muse of tragedy, on either side of satirical poetry. Garlands of flowers, brightened by the gold from the frames, run along the coving, going from a Muse to an allegory. Although the tapestries currently visible were not chosen by Fouquet – his were confiscated by the king –, they nonetheless date from the mid-seventeenth century and were woven after cartoons by Toussaint Dubreuil.

Thalia or Comedy
This detail of the coving gives some concept of Charles Le Brun's virtuosity; fresh back from Italy, he had brought with him from that country a kind of sensuous gaiety: Thalia, the muse of Comedy, her breast bared, is holding a mask in her hand. Flowers and vine leaves are twined round the trophies. Grouped in pairs at the corners of the coving, the Muses frame the four categories of poetry represented by en camaïeu figures, with the two medallions featuring Nobility and Peace.

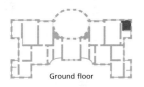

THE CABINET DES JEUX

*Ceiling of the Cabinet
des Jeux*
*While we do not know
who carried out the decoration
of the wainscoting and
the vaulting, the ceiling is
unquestionably the work
of Charles Le Brun.
The languorous figure on
the clouds is the very picture
of Sleep, the title of the work
which inspired La Fontaine
to write these few lines from
the Songe de Vaux :*

*"Held up in confort by
a breath of air so calm
Her arm upon a cloud,
her head upon the arm,
The flowers fall from her
hand, will not be disciplined
But gently slow about with
every passing wind
How beautiful she seems
to me, this sleeping Nigth."*

The Cabinet des Jeux
*This bright, cheerful little room
which was part of Fouquet's
apartment stands out less
for its size than for the quality
of its decoration, exceptional in
its detail. On the wainscoting,
between the gilding carried
out by Goujon known as La
Baronnière, one of Le Brun's
collaborators, there is a host
of putti, garlands and animals
against a light background.
Among the most frequently
recurring motifs: Fouquet's
squirrel, and the tower, the
heraldic emblem of his wife,
Marie-Madeleine de Castille.
Other animals can also be
seen, lizards, toads, peacocks
or butterflies, likewise with
a specific meaning,
the decoration as a whole
representing a real riddle.*

Detail of the coving
*The presence of the Fouquet
squirrel here is not surprising.
On the other hand the presence
of the grass snake apparently
threatening it has intrigued
historians, as that animal features*
*in the coat of arms of Colbert,
who was responsible for the
Superintendent's downfall. Might
it have been introduced into the
decoration subsequently, and if
so by whom? Or was Fouquet
assigning it a meaning that had*
*nothing to do with his enemy's
heraldic symbol? Although this
little mystery has not been
cleared up, it is hard to imagine
that the confrontation of these
two highly symbolic small animals
is due purely to chance.*

THE ANTICHAMBRE D'HERCULE

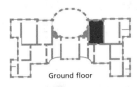

Ceiling of the Antichambre d'Hercule
This ceiling by Charles Le Brun depicts the apotheosis of Hercules, a theme the painter had previously treated in Paris at the Hôtel Lambert. On the left in the sky we see Jupiter, Juno and Diana welcoming Hercules to Olympus and on the right he is crowned by Victory; watched by Fame; Reason holds the horse's reins which symbolise the passions, while the wheels of the chariot crush Vice. In the side panels, four of the labours of Hercules are featured en camaieu, and they are continued in the medallions on the coving.

Antichambre d'Hercule
The antechamber to Fouquet's apartment, this room with its Italianate style owes its name to the iconography of the ceiling where the coving depicts the life of Hercules, the symbol of strength, a clear reference to the Superintendent's success and power. The same theme is repeated on the decoration of the panelling where Hercules' club, Apollo's lyre and Fouquet's monogram are associated.
While the set of tapestries depicting the Story of Clytemnestra which adorned the walls has gone, two marble-topped tables on carved legs which belonged to the Superintendent are still there, and have never left the château. On the wall, the Siege of Fribourg, a painting commissioned from Jean-Baptiste Martin by Field Marshal de Villars.

Seated nymph
This preparatory drawing was not conceived specifically for this room: Charles Le Brun, who before coming to Vaux had worked on the decoration of two Parisian houses, the Hôtel Lambert and the Hôtel La Rivière, reused it for another figure, the Juno we see in one of the compartments of the ceiling vaulting.

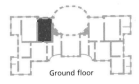

Corner of the coving
Above the gilt stucco shell the monogram of the Fouquets can be seen, traversed by an arrow, in a medallion framed by two putti in high relief.

Ceiling of the king's antechamber
The central motif of the present ceiling, a fresco, no doubt dates from the nineteenth century, but we do not know what Le Brun intended to put on this surface, as no trace has been handed down to us. The main ceiling panel is edged by pairs of gilded squirrels, linked to one another by means of a garland.

The king's antechamber
This room which was turned into a library in the eighteenth century by the duc de Choiseul-Praslin formed part of the king's apartment; it was obviously not finished in Fouquet's day. Even so it is outstanding for its Italianate covings which are attributed to Jean Cotelle: trompe-l'œil paintings alternate with gilded relief stucco decorations, frames and putti. In the medallions in the coving above the fire-place wall we see Achilles asking Venus to hand back the shield stolen by Cupid, and opposite Diana removing her shoes after the chase; above the windows, Cupid carrying Jupiter's thunderbolt, and on the wall opposite, Cupid carrying a vine plant pursued by a lion.

As regards the furniture, the mahogany book shelves in Louis XVI style have been complemented by an outstanding Boulle desk in six legs. The armchairs from the French Regency period are embellished with petit point tapestries.

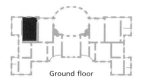

**Ceiling and coving
of the king's room**
The centre of the ceiling,
executed by Charles Le Brun,
is occupied by the Triumph
of Truth supported by Time.
In the side covings, at the top
of this photograph, Vertumnus
or Abundance, at the bottom
Mercury or Vigilance; Jupiter
or Power and Mars or Valour
are featured on either side.
At the corners, the octagonal
en camaïeu medallions depict
Leda, Diana, the Fates and
equestrian battles. However,
it is not very clear what all
these iconographic elements
signify. The ceiling cornice
is emphasised by gilded
palmettes, featuring a squirrel
and a tower alternately.

The king's room
The tradition of keeping
a suite of rooms intended for
a possible visit from the king,
inherited from the period when
monarchs led a semi-nomadic
existence, was preserved in
many grand houses: such visits
were latterly fairly rare, and no
French king ever slept at Vaux.
Nonetheless it explains the
decorative richness of such
rooms: this particular one,
in the Baroque style, with its
very heavy ceiling and its
paintings, did not break with
the tradition, and anticipates
Versailles. Here again Le Brun
was in charge of the decorative
programme, and the drawings
have been preserved.
The alcove, its limits bounded
by a gilded balustrade, houses
a bed with two Boulle chests
of drawers, one on either side,
comparable to those made
in 1705 for Louis XIV's
bedchamber at the Trianon,
then at Versailles. Above the
alcove, the coving is painted
with a representation of
Vertumnus

Winged stucco figure
In the covings winged stucco
figures and putti can be seen,
the work of Girardon and
Legendre.

Ceiling of the Duchess de Villars' private room
The decoration of this ceiling is not Jean Cotelle's only achievement at Vaux: the decoration of Fouquet's bedroom on the first-floor is also attributed to him. This remarkable ornamenter, a pupil of Simon Vouet and a member of the Académie from 1651, had already worked for the king at the Louvre and the Tuileries, and we are familiar with many engravings of his schemes which bear witness to the exceptional richness of his resourcefulness.

Duchesse de Villars'
private room
This room, formerly the king's
study, was not completed, and
should have received a painted
decoration. It also displays
a bronze bust of Villars,
and a portrait of Louis XV –

Villars was his Constable –,
Marie-Angélique de
Varengeville by Charles
Coypel, and the outstanding
Visit of Queen Marie Leczynska
to Vaux in 1728, a unique
painting depicting Vaux-
le-Vicomte.

Cupola in the bathroom
Although according to reports the
upkeep of the château was relatively
neglected in the early nineteenth
century, duc Charles de Praslin did
attempt some partial renovations,
turning to the architect Louis Visconti
for help. It was Visconti who in 1834-
1836 carried out the decoration of
the bathroom ceiling, which is circular
in shape, taking his inspiration from
the seventeenth-century decorations.

**Field Marshal de Villars'
study**

*This room which led into the
Field Marshal's bedroom is
painted with trompe-l'œil
woodwork. As well as a copy
of the portrait of the Villars by
Hyacinthe Rigaud, we see a
medallion depicting Louis XIV
on the wall, framed by two
bronze busts: on the left the
Prince de Condé, on the right
Field Marshal de Turenne by
Antoine Coysevox. The drawers
of the huge Louis XIV armoire
still to this day contain all Field
Marshal de Villars' archives.*

The wife of Field Marshal de Villars by Charles Coypel, detail
This allegorical portrait embellishing Field Marshal de Villars' antechamber is a completely typical example of the graceful style fashionable in the reign of Louis XV, with garlands interwoven with putti and Apollo appearing to listen in delight to the perfect notes of the young woman's lute.

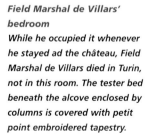

Field Marshal de Villars' bedroom
While he occupied it whenever he stayed ad the château, Field Marshal de Villars died in Turin, not in this room. The tester bed beneath the alcove enclosed by columns is covered with petit point embroidered tapestry.

Field Marshal de Villars after Hyacinthe Rigaud
Hector de Villars who was very proud of his success commissioned the very artist who was painter to Louis XIV to paint his portrait.

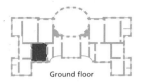
DINING-ROOM

A compartment in the dining-room ceiling, and Old man, seated *by Charles Le Brun*
The painter has taken Winter, *treated in grisaille and occupying one of the coffers, from his preparatory drawing.*

Panel from the wainscoting in the dining-room
In the wainscoting in the dining-room we again find compositions where the squirrel of Fouquet and the tower with three crenellations of Marie-Madeleine de Castille are associated, here treated against a background of arabesques in the style of Raphaël's loggie *at the Vatican.*

Central motif of the dining-room ceiling
The coffered ceiling consisting of nine compartments has as its central motif a work by Charles Le Brun, Peace restoring Abundance, *believed to be a reference to the Peace of the Pyrenees (1659) negotiated by Mazarin. Surrounding it are representations of the four seasons* en camaïeu *in grey, and the four elements* en camaïeu *in gold and blue: Apollo or Fire, the Naiads or Water, Flora or Earth, Diana or Air.*

Serving area
As the idea of setting aside
a room for meals dates only
from the mid-seventeenth
century in France – they were
usually eaten on occasional
tables in small rooms –,
Fouquet proved innovative
in creating a dining-room.

It is complemented by
the serving area, a vaulted
room behind the arcade,
where dishes arriving from
the kitchens were kept warm.
Above both the arcade and
the mirror flowers and fruit
are depicted, intermingled with
the trophies of War and Peace.

Above the doors, six circular
or octagonal medallions
feature the story of Io,
pursued by the jealous hatred
of Juno. At the bottom of
the wainscoting with its
decoration of arabesques
we can see children's games
in grisaille.

Ceiling of the Superintendent's bedroom
This ceiling was probably designed and executed by Jean Cotelle. The central part is illustrated with an Apollo bringing light to the world, a symbol identified with Fouquet and already planed for the ground floor. Around this central motif, four mythological scenes, Diana and Actaeon, Diana and Calypso, Apollo and Marsyas, Apollo and the serpent Python, and four medallions featuring Jupiter, Juno, Neptune and Cybele en camaïeu *in blue.*

General view of Fouquet's bedroom
Of the first-floor apartments, only Fouquet's bedroom has retained its complete decoration. This is the room where he slept before his arrest and imprisonment, and it is from these same leaded windows that he viewed his domain for the last time. The tapestries on the walls which depict the Months *after Lucas de Leyde* had been commissioned by Fouquet himself: the originals, confiscated by Louis XIV and destroyed in 1787 so that the gold and silver threads could be recovered, had fortunately been copied by the Gobelins factory as early as the second half of the seventeenth century, and it is those copies that adorn the room. That is why the arms of the comte de Toulouse, a son of Louis XIV, and his wife Marie de Noailles are featured in the corners of these five tapestries.

Alcove ceiling
The alcove ceiling also makes use of trompe-l'œil, *here simulating a cupola with* cassoons, with Dawn and Dusk being depicted on either side.

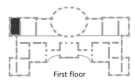

Beauty clipping Cupid's wings by Charles Le Brun
In this picture painted shortly after Fouquet's marriage to Marie-Madeleine de Castille in 1651, Le Brun has depicted an allegory of conjugal fidelity: assisted by Minerva or Wisdom and Hymen bearing a torch and a squirrel, Beauty, depicted with the features of the Superintendent's young wife, is clipping Cupid's wings to prevent him from taking flight. The historiographer André Félibien to whom we are indebted for many commentaries on the decoration of Vaux provided the key to this picture: *"Domestic love must not bear its arms beyond the home."*

Madame Fouquet's private room
It is to be regretted that the original decoration of this room, designed by Le Brun, has not been preserved: it would have provided interesting testimony of a fashion popular in the 1650s which involved covering walls with mirrors, anticipating the decoration of the Galerie des Glaces at Versailles. However, the lower wainscoting is original, while the doors come from another room in the château.

Casement window in Madame Fouquet's private room
This window overlooking the *parterres de broderie* has casements with clear glass panes set in lead cames, as they were originally. On either side, the wainscoting has been painted with arabesques.

Louis XV bedroom
Eighteenth-century style,
radically different from the
aesthetics of the century of
Louis XIV, is ideally represented
in this room. Straight lines and
pomp have been abandoned
in favour of curves, those
of the fireplace responding
to those of the furniture,
and the colours have become
fresher, imitating nature.
Although the majesty of gold
has not been completely
abandoned, as the tester bed
by Leroy demonstrates, there
was now a preference for
white and bright colours.

LOUIS XV DRESSING-ROOM
LOUIS XV BEDROOM

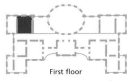

THE PRASLIN BEDROOM

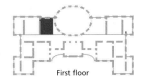

Louis XV dressing-room
As Field Marshal de Villars
had the layout of the rooms
altered, what had been
Madame Fouquet's bedroom
was divided into two to create
this dressing-room and
the following bedroom. The
eighteenth-century furniture
gives some insight into the
means used to meet the
concern with hygiene that
developed at that period.

The Praslin bedroom
Preferring smaller rooms that
were easier to heat and make
comfortable, in keeping with
the trend of the time, c. 1780
the Praslin family subdivided
what had been Madame
Fouquet's antechamber,
thus creating a bedroom,
a bathroom, an antechamber,
a servant's bedroom and
a water closet. The bedroom
from the Louis XV period
already heralded the style
of the Louis XVI period, with
its elegant, refined furniture,
though curved lines were now
absent. On the wall, a portrait
by Roslin of the duc de Praslin
who bought the Vaux estate.

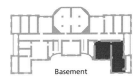
Basement

KITCHENS

The kitchens
The raised height of
the château in relation to
the level of the ground meant
that the kitchens could be
designed with high windows
open to the light, so avoiding
any impression of being in
an underground cellar.
The masonry work of the
brick vaults has remained
visible on some walls, while
others have been rendered.
Thanks to Le Vau's plans
which have been preserved,
we know the original purpose
of each of these rooms: cellars
and stores for wine, fruit,
preserves and bread-making,
a kitchen for special dishes,
a servants' hall, rooms for
"officials", those in charge
of aspects of service, etc.
The vaulted rooms in the
basement, the larders in
particular, were designed
to ensure that food would
keep well; ice brought from
the ice-store located outside
the château was also used for
this purpose – a well where
blocks of ice were piled up
during severe frosts. It was

blocked off with plaster,
so ensuring that the ice
remained frozen until autumn.
Various types of fire were used
in these kitchens: an open
fireplace which meant food
could be spit-roasted, ovens
and cooking ranges for cooking
by charcoal. Thanks to the cook

books of the period published
at this time, we can have a
very clear idea of the dishes
served at Fouquet's table:
he was one of the instigators
of French grande cuisine.
An army of servants filled
the basement with life,
under the supervision of

a major-domo. Fouquet's
major-domo was the famous
Vatel, who committed suicide
a few years later when in
the service of the Condé family,
on the pretext that the fish
had not arrived in time.
The big kitchen at Vaux has
been in virtually uninterrupted

use since Fouquet's day: it was
refitted in 1875, and was used
daily until 1956.

The outbuildings seen from the moat
The outbuildings, intended as servants' lodgings, stables, barns and workshops, also include a chapel. They form two symmetrical groups on either side of a beaten earth forecourt at the entrance to the château. Apparently work started on them even before the main house was built, but they were unfinished when Fouquet was sent to prison. Each part is comprised of a courtyard, enclosed by elongated buildings and pavilions, one being the chapel courtyard and the other the stables courtyard. Unlike the château, built entirely of stone, these buildings have course work of brick and stone, while some are constructed of rendered quarry stones. As for the roofs, the slope visible from the château is covered with slate, the other slope with flat tiles.

Façade of the garden side of the outbuildings overlooking the stables courtyard
The initial purpose of this building is not known for certain, but it was used as an orangery in the nineteenth century. It is probable that Vaux, like all noble residences, did have an orangery in the seventeenth century, but it may well have been a temporary building used during the cold season, then destroyed.

Façade of the outbuildings overlooking the forecourt
On the left of these buildings that run along the chapel courtyard, we can see a large pavilion with a mansard roof, the three arches on its façade forming a symmetrical effect with the monumental portico to the right leading into the forest. Between them there are two more unassuming pavilions.

The farm
An estate as large as Vaux justified agricultural activities and buildings earmarked for them. The two courtyards included two identical rustic buildings, no doubt farms: the buildings depicted here were a working farm until quite recently.

The railings

Running between a series of terms, carved with double faces in the antique manner by Mathieu Lespagnandel, the railings enclosing the entrance to the château were still a novelty at the time. It was in fact in the mid-seventeenth century that large stone gateways and walls were abandoned when castles were built in favour of an open view along the axis of the entrance, provided by railings. On either side of the central wrought-iron gate, the two rusticated side gates seem to have been mock entrances, but they contribute to the harmony of the enclosure. Ironwork abounds at Vaux, since as well as the entrance gates, the railings embellishing the monumental false gates and the railings between the main garden and the kitchen garden, it was also used in the vestibule, the Grand Salon and the stairs. The work required was sufficiently extensive to justify establishing forges at Maincy.

Following double page:
View of garden
The parterres de broderie in the foreground lead the eye towards the grotto, dominated by the Hercules Farnese at the rear, placed there by Le Nôtre as the point of convergence for every perspective.

Plan of the gardens
This manuscript plan of the gardens, which does not in fact totally correspond with what was done, was probably established by Le Nôtre on his arrival c. 1653. However, though we are indebted to him for the final harmony of the parterres and fountains, the landscaping of the site had been started well before, probably in 1641 when Fouquet purchased the estate. For the plot of ground had to be remodelled and planted up a very long time before work started on building the house; it was necessary to make skilful use of the stream that ran into the river Anqueuil – the winding course of the stream can be seen on the left of the plan – to feed the ponds and the moats.

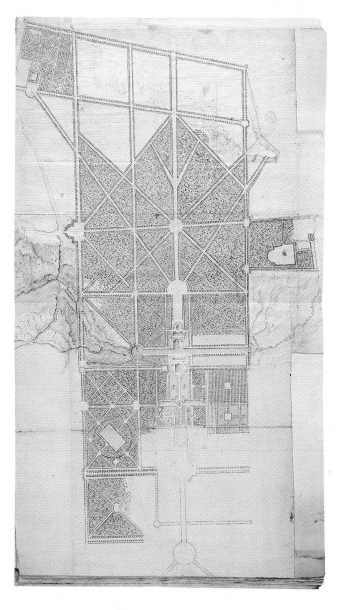

View of the château from the Carré d'eau
Since the Renaissance, the subtle association of natural setting and architecture in Italian gardens had inspired deep admiration in France, which even in the sixteenth century prompted the creation of some outstanding gardens such as those at Anet and Blois. If the ground itself had no marked contours, an area had to be created in which different levels would allow for unexpected perspectives, running water, and mysterious set pieces: this is what interested Fouquet as he studied engravings of the plans of Italian, English or German gardens, visited the gardens at Rueil or Meudon, and associated with the circle of artists centred on the painter Simon Vouet, of which André Le Nôtre formed part. Le Nôtre, who became head gardener at Vaux, himself came from a family of gardeners.

Parterre de broderie in front of the château
Behind this bed with its delicate coating of frost, reinstated by Achille Duchêne in 1923, we can see the Rond d'eau on the left, with four statues dating from the seventeenth century encircling it. Lower down, at the bottom of some steps watched over by lions and tigers sculpted by Gardet, is the third level of the garden: on either side of the Allée d'eau, in the centre of the turfed-over beds, the Bassins des Tritons.

FOUNTAINS

*View of the Grille d'eau,
drawing by Israël Silvestre*
This seventeenth-century
drawing enables us to note
some small changes to the
Grille d'eau made between
the period of Fouquet and
today, in particular the fact
that the fountain was in
working order since we can see
water gushing up vertically
between the two terms.

The Gerbe
In the central axis the Bassin
de la Gerbe, located above the
Grotto, dominates the gardens
and is their apotheosis: its name
comes from the powerful jet
– or "sheaf" – of water over
three metres high which used
to rise from it, as can be seen
on Israël Silvestre's drawings
and engravings.

Visit of Queen Marie Leczynska to Vaux in 1728
In this picture of the gardens at Vaux at the beginning of the eighteenth century in the reign of Louis XV, we can see all the water effects in play, more particularly the waterfalls and the 'Gerbe', the circular pool that can be seen in the foreground, behind the figures on horseback.

Pool in the parterres beside the Allée d'eau
After the Rond d'eau, a pool marking the mid-point of the garden, the main axis is known as the Allée d'eau (waterway path) because of the "bubbles" forming a liquid hedge that used to line it. They have not been reinstated, and have been replaced by box hedges. At the centre of the parterres on either side there are pools decorated with nineteenth-century sculptures by Émile Peynot, tritons surrounded by children and naiads, commissioned by Alfred Sommier after he bought the château.

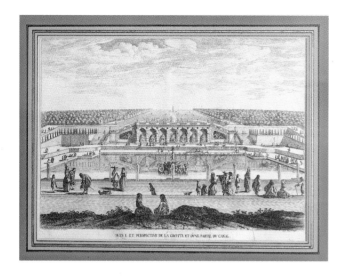

View of the Grotto from the waterfalls, drawing by Israël Silvestre
As the garden was designed on several levels, in this drawing we cannot see the waterfalls, which can be inferred only from the vertical spouts of water emerging from them. Beyond them in the centre of the Carré d'eau, which can be reached along two paths forming a horseshoe shape, a statue of Neptune which has now disappeared used to sit enthroned above the sculpted group. Still farther away is the Grotto, with a balustrade above it where figures can be seen, and at the end of the axis the silhouetted figure of Hercules; Le Nôtre planned this arrangement, but the current replica was not installed until the nineteenth century. The low stature of the trees lining the central axis allows us to surmise that they had been planted relatively recently.

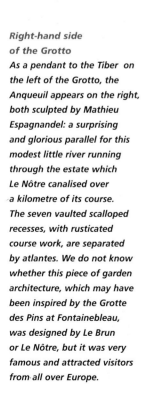

Right-hand side of the Grotto
As a pendant to the Tiber on the left of the Grotto, the Anqueuil appears on the right, both sculpted by Mathieu Espagnandel: a surprising and glorious parallel for this modest little river running through the estate which Le Nôtre canalised over a kilometre of its course. The seven vaulted scalloped recesses, with rusticated course work, are separated by atlantes. We do not know whether this piece of garden architecture, which may have been inspired by the Grotte des Pins at Fontainebleau, was designed by Le Brun or Le Nôtre, but it was very famous and attracted visitors from all over Europe.

GROTTO

View from the flights of steps leading to the Grotto
The full harmony of the horizontal planes can be appreciated in this view which finishes in the distance with the lantern roof of the château. The movement of the stairs and ramps which dominate the Grotto, reminiscent of Saint-Germain-en-Laye, is visibly inspired by Italian examples, in particular by the Villa d'Este at Tivoli. Below the ramp, two lions sculpted by Mathieu Espagnandel are holding a squirrel and a cornucopia between their paws.

The Canal
*Behind the group of children
and sea-horses sculpted
by Alfred Lanson in 1880
runs the peaceful canal.
At considerable expense,
Fouquet had the course
of the Anqueil altered
by forty-five degrees and
it was canalised over a length
of one kilometre. Cutting
the garden along a transversal
axis and widened at the foot
of the waterfalls, this canal
ends in a pool known as
the Poële (frying-pan) because
of its circular shape. As can
be seen from some engravings,
there used to be boating
on the canal; the boats then
turned in this pool to retrace
the same route.*

The torrent
*Located where two valleys
converge, the Vaux estate
had two water courses
available for use: the Anqueil,
which was canalised, and
a small stream running into it.
Captured and made to run
underground, the stream fed
the moats and ponds before
flowing into the canal, forming
a little waterfall known
as the torrent.*

The canal
*This view of the canal with
the dark trees reflected in
it is a perfect illustration
of the harmonious marriage
of nature and built stone
sought by Le Nôtre, running
through the very different,
but always soothing
atmospheres from one end
of the gardens to the other.*

SCULPTURES

Cupids bearing a basket
This little seventeenth-century group which Fouquet would not have disdained was not sculpted for Vaux, but for the château of Maisons: attributed to Philippe de Buyster, it was purchased with three other identical ones by Alfred Sommier in the nineteenth century to replace statues that had disappeared from the gardens. Among them were eleven terms designed by Nicolas Poussin which Louis XIV had sent to Versailles.

The abduction of Europa
Perched on her bull, this Europa sculpted by Ernest-Eugène Hiolle in 1886 reverts to a theme often illustrated at the period when the château was built.

View of the Grille d'eau
At the end of the transversal axis the Grille d'eau rises, forming a symmetrical counterpart to the railings of the kitchen garden; before it is a terrace where on 17 August 1661 Molière put on a performance of Les Fâcheux in the illuminated gardens. In the background the two bifacial terms representing the seasons of life date from 1661, but at that time there were human figures instead of dogs – the work of Michel Anguier – on the side plinths. The mascarons adorning the levels of the Grille d'eau feature various representations of fauns, satyrs and goat-footed creatures, conjuring up the woodland deities.

LES AMIS DE   VAUX LE VICOMTE

The association "Les Amis de Vaux-le-Vicomte" which brings together those whose aim it is to preserve the high standards of this private estate was created in 1983.

It's objectives are defined in article 2 of the statutes :

"to contribute to the maintainance and restoration of the château, the outbuildings and gardens of Vaux-le-Vicomte located in Seine-et-Marne (France) which have been listed as Historical Monuments,"

"to upkeep the art collections presently housed at Vaux-le-Vicomte or which may be housed there on a permanent basis ; to receive or acquire any art objects, souvenirs, documents either connected with Vaux-le-Vicomte and those families that have contributed to its creation and maintenance, or any works of art to be kept at Vaux-le-Vicomte,"

"to encourage public visits, subject to any special circumstances and all requirements connected with the conservation and restoration of the site,"

"to undertake all actions for the encouragement of the Arts by all appropriate means, to promote visits by students and researchers interested in the subjects offered by Vaux-le-Vicomte,"

"to organize or help organize meetings, exhibits, publications or to undertake or further the undertaking of studies."

For subscription forms and information, please apply to estate Office :
Vaux-le-Vicomte - 77950 Maincy - France
Tel : (33) 01 64 14 41 90 - Fax : (33) 01 60 69 90 85
Internet : http:\www.vaux-le-vicomte.com
E-mail : chateau@vaux-le-vicomte.com

This tapestry, one of a series of five representing the History of Diane the huntress *after the cartoons by Toussaint Dubreuil (1633) was purchased by the association of Friends of Vaux-le-Vicomte in 1994.*

Text by Anne SEFRIOUI
Layout: Frédéric CELESTIN and Thierry RENARD
© ÉDITIONS SCALA, Paris
ISBN 2-86656-190-2
Printed in Italy by EDITORIALE

All the photographs are by Georges FESSY,
except p. 8t, 12t, 12b, 27b, 32br, 38bl, 112t © RMN Paris ; p. 9t and 49tr
© Bnf, Paris ; p. 55t © Bibliothèque de l'Institut de France, Paris